Stitch
-by-
Stitch

JANE BULL

DK

Design and Text Jane Bull
Photographer Andy Crawford
US Senior editor Shannon Beatty
US editor Margaret Parrish
Senior editor Carrie Love
Editors Alexander Cox, Lee Wilson
Designers Victoria Palastanga,
Lauren Rosier
Production editor Dragana Puvacic
Production controller Inderjit Bhullar
Managing editor Penny Smith
Deputy art editor Mabel Chan
Publishing director Sarah Larter

This American Edition, 2023
First American Edition, 2012
Published in the United States by DK Publishing
1745 Broadway, 20th Floor, New York,
New York 10019

Copyright © 2012, 2017, 2023
Dorling Kindersley Limited
DK, a Division of Penguin Random House LLC
23 24 25 26 27 10 9 8 7 6 5 4 3 2
002–336960–Nov/2023

Copyright © 2012, 2017, 2023 Jane Bull

A catalog record for this book is available from the
Library of Congress.
ISBN 978-0-7440-8638-6

DK books are available at special discounts when
purchased in bulk for sales promotions, premiums,
fund-raising, or educational use. For details, contact:
DK Publishing Special Markets, 1745 Broadway,
20th Floor, New York, NY 10019
SpecialSales@dk.com
Printed in China

For the curious
www.dk.com

MIX
Paper | Supporting
responsible forestry
FSC™ C018179

This book was made with Forest
Stewardship Council™ certified
paper - one small step in DK's
commitment to a sustainable future.
For more information go to
www.dk.com/our-green-pledge

Contents

Before you begin

NOTE TO CHILDREN
The projects in this book are fun to create, but make sure you follow the instructions carefully. Always take extra care with any needles and embroidery scissors, since they are sharp. Ask an adult to cut fabric with dressmakers' scissors.

You can place a needle in a pincushion to stop it from moving when you are threading it to prevent any accidental needle jabs.

When using pins, keep a pincushion nearby, and stick them back into it when you are done. Gather up any pins that have fallen on the floor. You can use a magnet for this, but never put a magnet in your mouth.

Ask an adult for help if a project gets too tricky. Let them do any ironing.

Be extra careful when using knitting needles. Do not injure yourself or others around you!

NOTE TO ADULTS
Please supervise your child, especially a younger one, during these projects. You know your child's dexterity and level of skill, and may need to adjust the tools accordingly (for example, by using a tapestry needle). Guide them on how to carry out the activities and allow them to do the steps that are more manageable.

Sewing basics

All the projects in *Stitch-by-Stitch* will need a handy kit like this, as well as the materials and equipment required for a particular technique. You will also need to know some basic sewing skills to complete the projects.

Sewing box

You can buy a sewing box to store all your sewing equipment and materials, but why not make one out of a shoebox instead?

Handy tip

Remember to keep this kit with you when making the projects in this book.

Thread

It's handy to have a selection of sewing threads in different colors so you can match them to the fabrics you use. Needle threaders are useful.

Needles,

Sewing needles are usually thin with either a small eye or a long, thin eye. Keep a selection of needles in a needle case.

Pins

You'll need pins in a lot of the sewing projects. A pincushion keeps your pins safe and always on hand. Glass-headed pins are pretty and easy to see when dropped.

SEWING THREAD

NEEDLE THREADER

NEEDLE CASE

EMBROIDERY SCISSORS

PINCUSHION

DRESSMAKERS' SCISSORS

TAPE MEASURE

THIMBLE

Scissors

It helps to have good sharp scissors and the right ones for the job. Embroidery scissors are best for snipping threads and dressmakers' scissors are best for cutting larger pieces of fabric.

Thimble

You wear a thimble on the middle finger of the hand that is holding the needle. It is used to push the needle through the fabric and stops your finger from getting sore.

Tape measure

Some projects will have thread, fabric, and yarn that need accurate measuring.

Threading a needle

Threading a needle can be difficult. A needle with a larger eye will make it easier, or use a needle threader. Use sharp scissors to cut the thread.

Thread length?
If you work with thread that is too long it will get tangled, slowing you down. Cut a piece of thread roughly the length from your fingertips to your elbow.

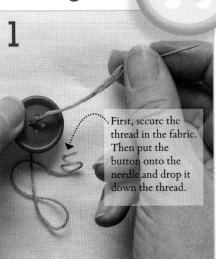

Thread the needle.

Double up the thread and knot the end.

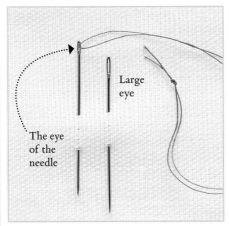

Large eye

The eye of the needle

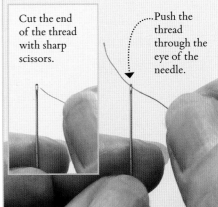

Cut the end of the thread with sharp scissors.

Push the thread through the eye of the needle.

USING A NEEDLE THREADER

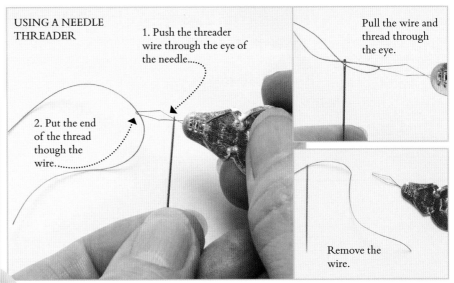

1. Push the threader wire through the eye of the needle.

2. Put the end of the thread though the wire.

Pull the wire and thread through the eye.

Remove the wire.

Sewing on a button

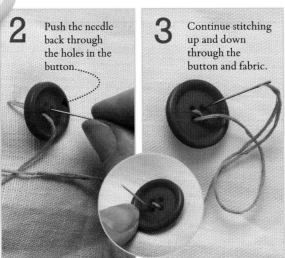

1

First, secure the thread in the fabric. Then put the button onto the needle and drop it down the thread.

2

Push the needle back through the holes in the button.

3

Continue stitching up and down through the button and fabric.

4

To secure the button, bring the thread up under the button.

Sew backward and forward behind the button, then cut the thread.

Sewing stitches

Here are the stitches that are used for the projects. They all have a different job to do when you are joining fabric together for cushions, bags, and patchwork pieces.

How to start and finish

Begin stitching with a knot at the end of the thread. To end a row of stitches, make a tiny stitch, but do not pull it tight. Bring the thread back up through the loop and pull tight. Do this once more in the same spot, then cut the thread.

Running stitch

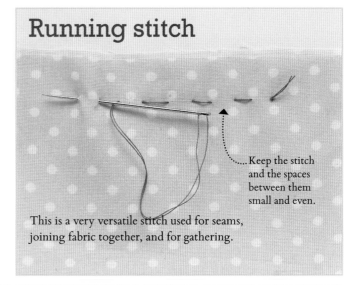

Keep the stitch and the spaces between them small and even.

This is a very versatile stitch used for seams, joining fabric together, and for gathering.

Backstitch

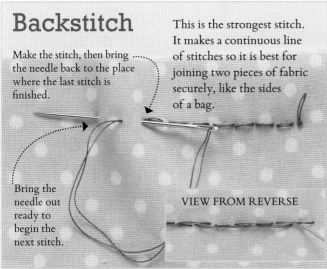

Make the stitch, then bring the needle back to the place where the last stitch is finished.

This is the strongest stitch. It makes a continuous line of stitches so it is best for joining two pieces of fabric securely, like the sides of a bag.

Bring the needle out ready to begin the next stitch.

VIEW FROM REVERSE

Basting stitch

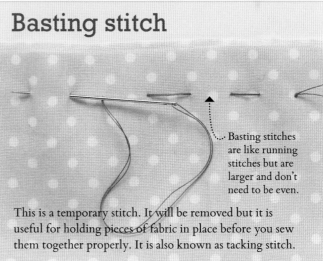

Basting stitches are like running stitches but are larger and don't need to be even.

This is a temporary stitch. It will be removed but it is useful for holding pieces of fabric in place before you sew them together properly. It is also known as tacking stitch.

Whipstitch

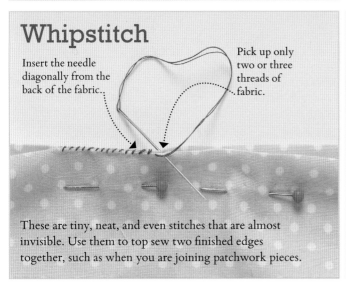

Insert the needle diagonally from the back of the fabric.

Pick up only two or three threads of fabric.

These are tiny, neat, and even stitches that are almost invisible. Use them to top sew two finished edges together, such as when you are joining patchwork pieces.

Slip stitch

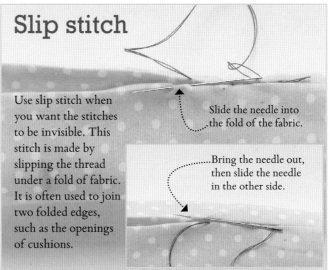

Slide the needle into the fold of the fabric.

Bring the needle out, then slide the needle in the other side.

Use slip stitch when you want the stitches to be invisible. This stitch is made by slipping the thread under a fold of fabric. It is often used to join two folded edges, such as the openings of cushions.

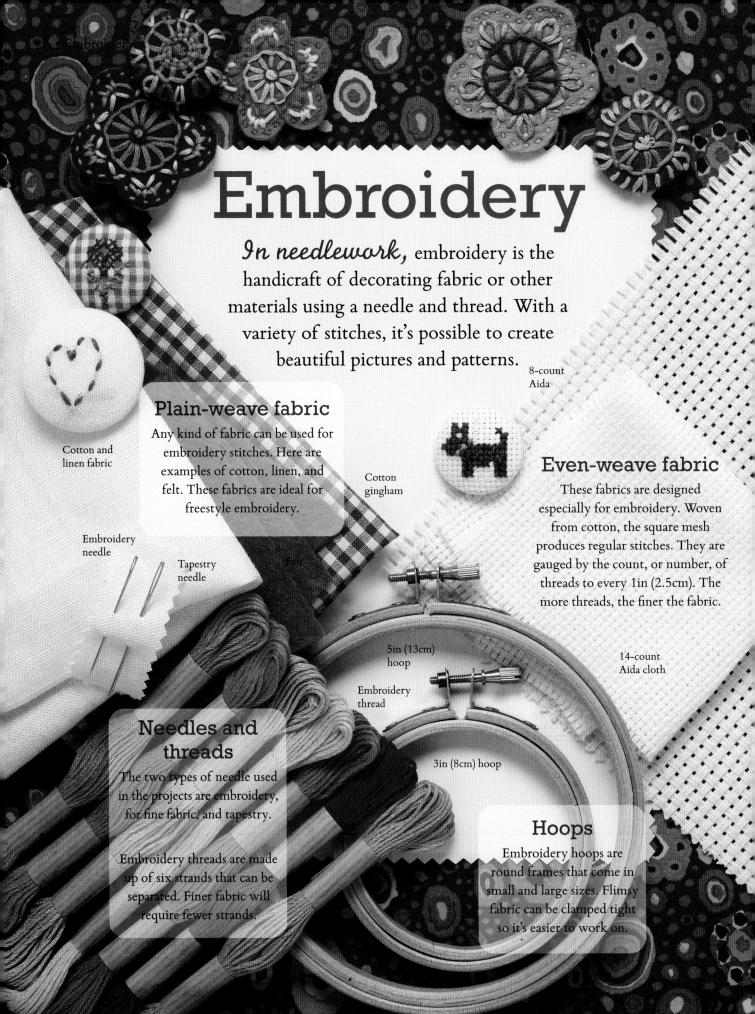

Embroidery

In needlework, embroidery is the handicraft of decorating fabric or other materials using a needle and thread. With a variety of stitches, it's possible to create beautiful pictures and patterns.

Plain-weave fabric

Any kind of fabric can be used for embroidery stitches. Here are examples of cotton, linen, and felt. These fabrics are ideal for freestyle embroidery.

Cotton and linen fabric

Embroidery needle

Tapestry needle

Cotton gingham

Felt

8-count Aida

Even-weave fabric

These fabrics are designed especially for embroidery. Woven from cotton, the square mesh produces regular stitches. They are gauged by the count, or number, of threads to every 1in (2.5cm). The more threads, the finer the fabric.

14-count Aida cloth

5in (13cm) hoop

Embroidery thread

3in (8cm) hoop

Needles and threads

The two types of needle used in the projects are embroidery, for fine fabric, and tapestry.

Embroidery threads are made up of six strands that can be separated. Finer fabric will require fewer strands.

Hoops

Embroidery hoops are round frames that come in small and large sizes. Flimsy fabric can be clamped tight so it's easier to work on.

Designs on even-weave fabric

Here is an example to show how the different counted thread affects the design. Notice how the same motif, using the same amount of stitches, changes size.

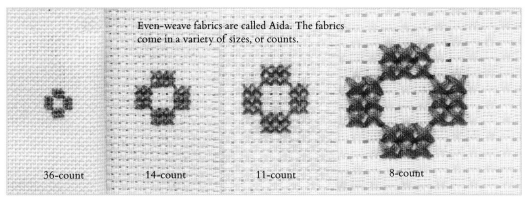

Even-weave fabrics are called Aida. The fabrics come in a variety of sizes, or counts.

36-count 14-count 11-count 8-count

Transferring designs

EVEN-WEAVE FABRIC

For this type of fabric, designs are made up of squares, with each square representing a stitch.

The designs don't have rounded edges because of the squares, but curves can be made by "stepping" the squares. When transferring the design to the cloth, only draw the outline of the colors, not every stitch.

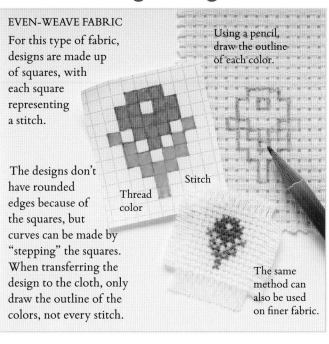

Using a pencil, draw the outline of each color.

Thread color

Stitch

The same method can also be used on finer fabric.

PLAIN-WEAVE FABRIC

For this type of fabric, any shape can be achieved, and it is ideal for freestyle stitching.

Drawings can be copied directly onto the fabric using a pencil. A ballpoint pen works well on darker fabrics.

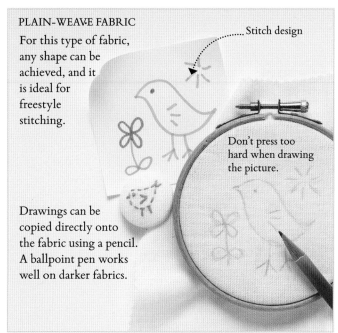

Stitch design

Don't press too hard when drawing the picture.

How to use a hoop

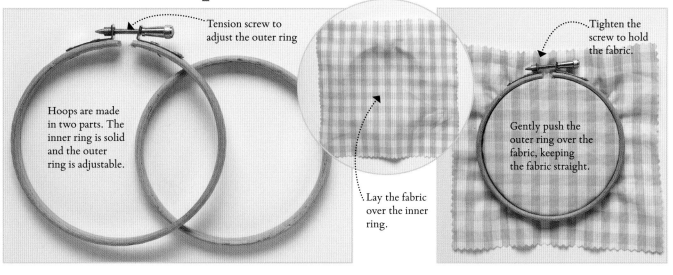

Tension screw to adjust the outer ring

Hoops are made in two parts. The inner ring is solid and the outer ring is adjustable.

Lay the fabric over the inner ring.

Tighten the screw to hold the fabric.

Gently push the outer ring over the fabric, keeping the fabric straight.

Stitches gallery

Running stitch

This stitch makes a dashed line. The stitches can vary in length, depending on the effect you want.

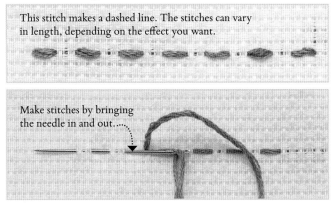

Make stitches by bringing the needle in and out....

Backstitch

Backstitch creates a continuous line.

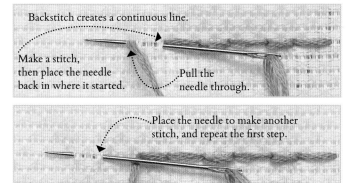

Make a stitch, then place the needle back in where it started.

Pull the needle through.

Place the needle to make another stitch, and repeat the first step.

Cross-stitch

"X" stitches can be worked in a row or on their own.

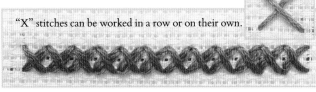

Stitch diagonal stitches in the same direction.

Bring the needle out here ready to begin the next stitch.

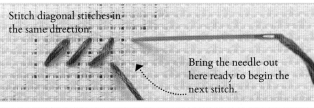

To complete the "X" shapes, work back across the row, using the same hole as the previous stitch.

Blanket stitch

This stitch is perfect for edging projects and for decoration.

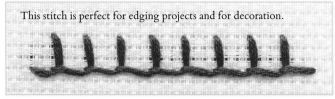

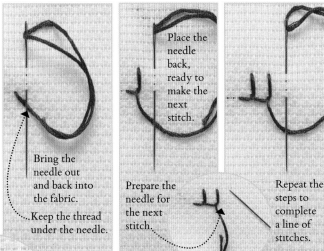

Bring the needle out and back into the fabric.

Keep the thread under the needle.

Place the needle back, ready to make the next stitch.

Prepare the needle for the next stitch.

Repeat the steps to complete a line of stitches.

Chain stitch

A decorative stitch with a chain effect.

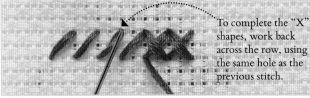

Single chains can look like leaves or petals.

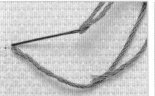

Bring the needle out and then put it back in next to the first stitch.

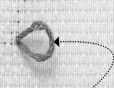

Pull the thread through until it forms a loop.

Bring the needle back up just inside the loop.

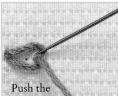

Push the needle back in next to the last stitch.

Make a new loop and repeat the steps to continue making a chain.

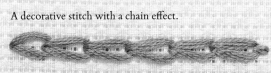

Crown stitch

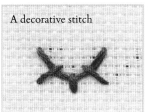
A decorative stitch

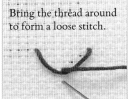
Bring the thread around to form a loose stitch.

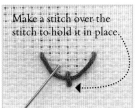
Make a stitch over the stitch to hold it in place.

Continue making stitches.

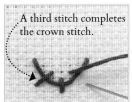
A third stitch completes the crown stitch.

French knot

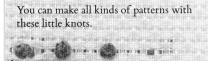
You can make all kinds of patterns with these little knots.

Wind the thread twice around the needle.

Push the needle back in close to the first stitch.

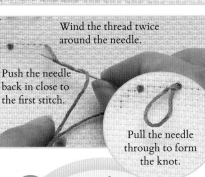
Pull the needle through to form the knot.

Handy tip

Cut a length of thread that is about the length from your fingertips to your elbow to avoid tangles and knots in the thread.

Threading a needle

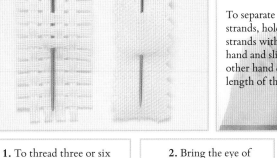
Tapestry needle   Embroidery needle

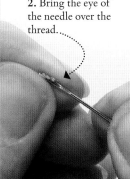
Separate the six strands.

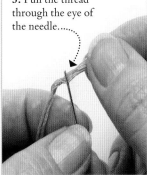
To separate the six strands, hold three strands with one hand and slide the other hand down the length of the thread.

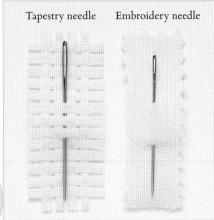

1. To thread three or six strands of thread, loop the thread over the needle and pull tight.

2. Bring the eye of the needle over the thread.

3. Pull the thread through the eye of the needle.

Starting and stopping

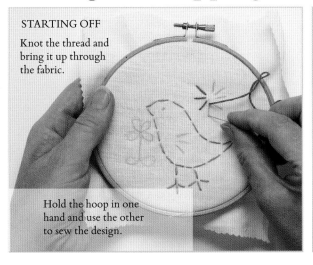

STARTING OFF

Knot the thread and bring it up through the fabric.

Hold the hoop in one hand and use the other to sew the design.

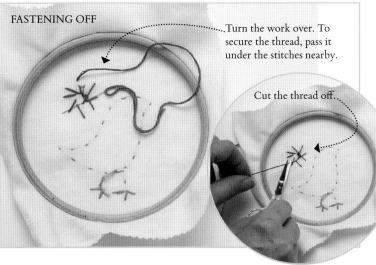

FASTENING OFF

Turn the work over. To secure the thread, pass it under the stitches nearby.

Cut the thread off.

Just by using simple stitches like blanket stitch, chain stitch, and straight stitch, you can make really colorful designs.

Felt flowers

To make a bunch of flowers, save all those pretty scraps of felt and transform them into bright and cheery blooms. Play with the colors of the felt and thread for dazzling effects.

You will need

- Colorful felt scraps
- Embroidery thread
- Embroidery needle

Attaching a pin to the back of the flower makes a charming brooch.

Small lengths of embroidery thread

Save small pieces of felt for projects like this.

Flower templates

Place tracing paper on top of these shapes and trace over them with pencil. Transfer the design onto thin cardboard. Cut out the cardboard and use the shapes for the felt flower.

See page 62 for transferring designs.

How to stitch a flower

To make a flower shape, first, lay the template on a piece of felt. Carefully draw around the edge of the cardboard and around the center. This will be a guide to show you where to start the flower center.

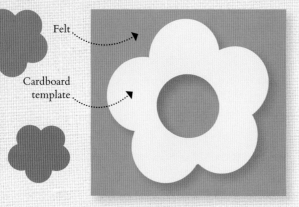

Felt

Cardboard template

You will need

Felt shape for backing

Felt shape for flower front

Embroidery needle

Embroidery threads in different colors

1 Start stitching the center of the flower.

Blanket stitch

2 Single chain stitch

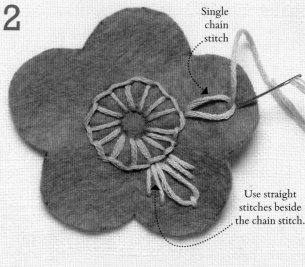

Use straight stitches beside the chain stitch.

3 Sew the front and back pieces together.

Running stitch

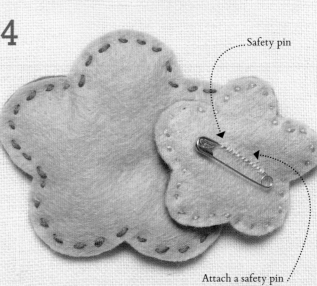

4 Safety pin

Attach a safety pin by sewing it to the back of the flower.

Cover button bases with your embroidery to create beautiful buttons.

Brighten up your T-shirts, jackets, and jeans with colorful stitches.

Sewing flowers on your clothes

Use the flower template to draw the pattern you want to sew. Then simply follow the steps for the felt flowers.

Choose where you want the stitching to go and mark the design out in the same way as on the felt.

Flower patch

Use the flowers as patches—sew them on to clothes and bags.

Pin a flower to the garment.

Sew the flower in position using a running stitch.

Decorated beany hat

Simple sampler

Try out your skills with a sampler. Traditionally, samplers were a way to practice your skills at embroidery. Here is an easy design of hearts and flowers to start with.

Frame your finished work.

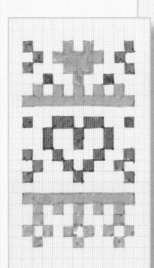

Each square represents a stitch and shows which color thread to use.

You will need

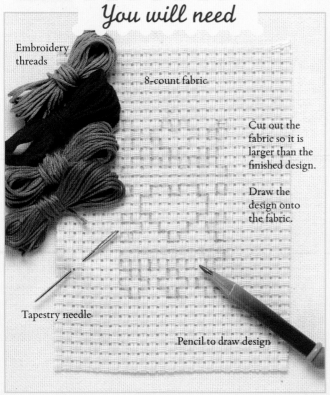

Embroidery threads

8-count fabric

Cut out the fabric so it is larger than the finished design.

Draw the design onto the fabric.

Tapestry needle

Pencil to draw design

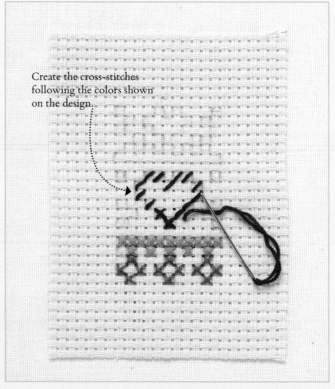

Create the cross-stitches following the colors shown on the design.

Good gifts

These homemade samplers make perfect gifts. Frame and attach some ribbon for hanging.

Make it larger

Use the alternative template to create a larger sampler. Remember, it's not necessary to draw the entire design onto the fabric; the first few rows will help as a guide.

Needlepoint

Also known as tapestry, or canvas work, needlepoint is the craft of stitching onto a firm, open-weave canvas. The stitches are worked on a canvas grid and tightly stitched so that none of the background is left showing.

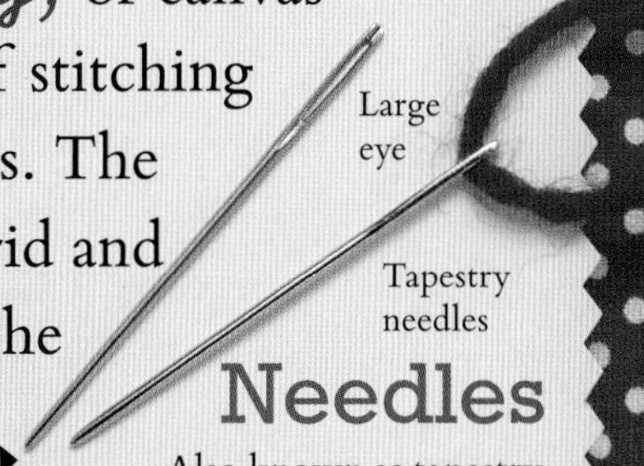

Rounded end

Large eye

Tapestry needles

Needles

Also known as tapestry needles, needlepoint needles have rounded ends. This helps to prevent the point from catching the canvas threads. The large eye makes it easy to thread.

Canvas

Canvas is made of cotton thread that has been treated to make it very stiff. It is sized by mesh sizes, or thread count per 1in (2.5cm); for example, "10 count" means there are 10 threads to 1in (2.5cm). The sizes range from 5 count to 24 count; the smaller the mesh, the finer the stitches will be. Canvas can be bought with a preprinted design in kits from craft stores, or plain in yard lengths.

The projects in this book use 10-count canvas— 10 threads to 1in (2.5cm).

Skeins of tapestry yarn

Projects

There are all kinds of needlepoint equipment and materials available, from plastic canvas to kits with printed designs. The items shown here are all you need to complete the projects that follow and to create your own designs, too.

Threads

Needlepoint thread comes in wool, cotton, or silk. Tapestry yarn gives the best results on 10-count canvas, as the woolen stitches lay close together, completely hiding the canvas underneath. You can buy it in measured lengths called skeins.

Cutting the canvas

Taping the edges is optional.

Before you start, cut out a piece of canvas. Count the number of stitches required for your design and then decide how much room to leave around the edge, as the canvas needs to be larger than your design. This border can be cut away later or kept if you want to frame your work.

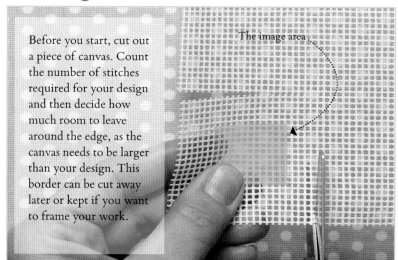

The image area

If the yarn keeps catching on the edge of the canvas, use masking tape to cover the edges.

Masking tape

Transferring designs

Needlepoint designs are made up of squares, with each square representing a stitch. Notice that the stitch doesn't go in the holes of the canvas, but across the threads. The design is just a guide. Create your own design using graph paper and some colored pens.

Design your own image on graph paper.

Graph paper

Copy the design onto the canvas, coloring the places the stitches will go.

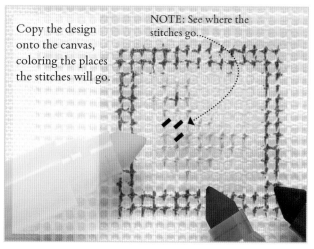

NOTE: See where the stitches go.

Threading a tapestry needle

Cut a piece of yarn 20in (50cm) long, thread the needle, and knot the end of the yarn.

Fold the end of the yarn over the needle and pull tight.

Pinch the loop between your fingers.

Put the eye of the needle over the loop.

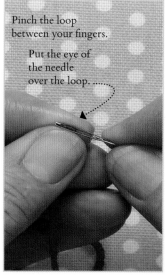

Slide the eye of the needle down the loop.

Pull the yarn through until the short end is out of the eye.

Begin stitching

These steps have been made using tent stitch.

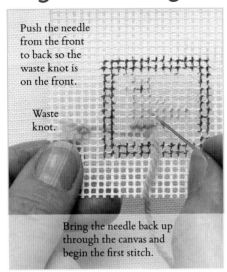

Push the needle from the front to back so the waste knot is on the front.

Waste knot.

Bring the needle back up through the canvas and begin the first stitch.

Continue stitching the same color forward and backward.

Keep the stitch facing in the same direction.

To finish a color, turn the work over and slide the needle under the stitches.

Pull the needle all the way through and then cut off the yarn.

Add new color

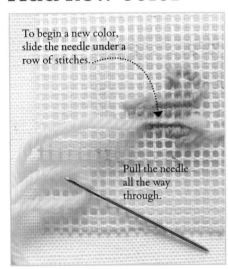

To begin a new color, slide the needle under a row of stitches.

Pull the needle all the way through.

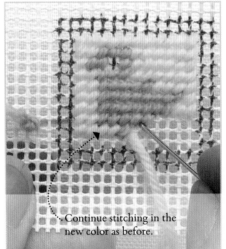

Continue stitching in the new color as before.

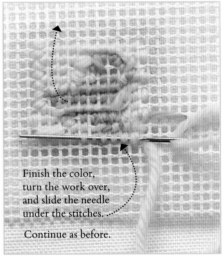

Finish the color, turn the work over, and slide the needle under the stitches.

Continue as before.

Finishing

Continue stitching the design following the pattern.

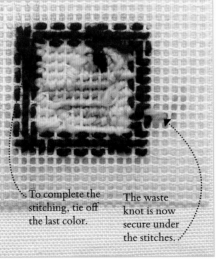

To complete the stitching, tie off the last color.

The waste knot is now secure under the stitches.

The waste knot can now be cut off.

Needlepoint stitches

Simple stitches Although there are lots of different styles of needlepoint stitches to choose from, here are four types of stitch to try in the projects that follow. The simplest is tent stitch, which is a small diagonal stitch. These examples of needlepoint show that by varying the size of the stitch, the direction it goes, and the color combinations, many patterns and designs can be achieved.

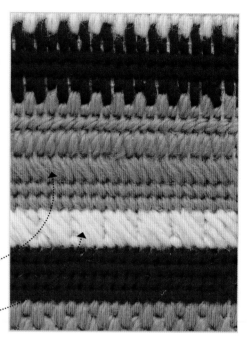

Interlocking straight stitch

Tent stitch

Diagonal stitch

Cushion stitch

DIAGONAL STITCH

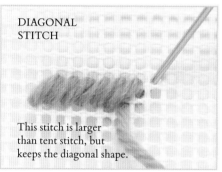

This stitch is larger than tent stitch, but keeps the diagonal shape.

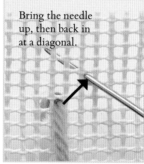

Bring the needle up, then back in at a diagonal.

Bring the needle back through the canvas to the front, next to the first stitch.

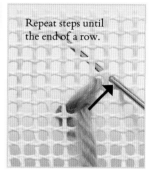

Repeat steps until the end of a row.

DIAGONAL SQUARE

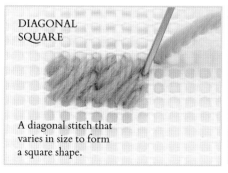

A diagonal stitch that varies in size to form a square shape.

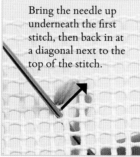

Bring the needle up underneath the first stitch, then back in at a diagonal next to the top of the stitch.

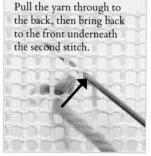

Pull the yarn through to the back, then bring back to the front underneath the second stitch.

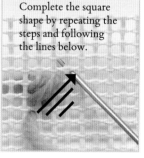

Complete the square shape by repeating the steps and following the lines below.

INTERLOCKING STRAIGHT STITCH

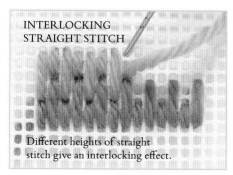

Different heights of straight stitch give an interlocking effect.

Bring the needle out of the canvas...

... then back into the canvas using a straight stitch.

Repeat these steps, alternating long and short straight stitches.

All squared

See how many patterns you can make by simply using squares. Try the designs shown here or figure out your own by drawing them on paper first. These cushions are ideal for pins, but they can be any size you like.

You will need

Canvas

Tapestry needle

Felt for backing

Stuffing for the cushion.

Sewing needle

Tapestry yarn

Cotton thread

How to make a cushion

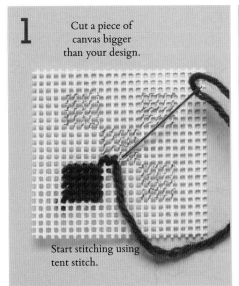

1 Cut a piece of canvas bigger than your design.

Start stitching using tent stitch.

2 When all the red is done, begin the second color.

3 Cut off the canvas, but DON'T cut too close to the stitching.

4 Sew over the edge of the canvas.

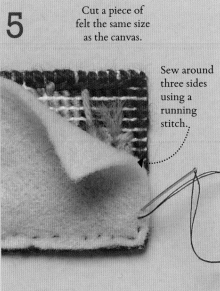

5 Cut a piece of felt the same size as the canvas.

Sew around three sides using a running stitch.

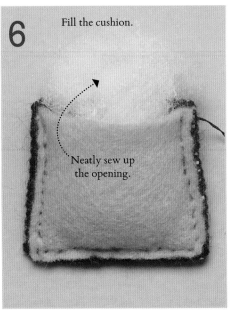

6 Fill the cushion.

Neatly sew up the opening.

The biggest cushion here is 4½in (11cm) x 4½in (11cm); the smallest is 1½in (4cm) x 1½in (4cm).

Pincushions

Rainbow frames

Canvas is a strong, stiff material, which makes it ideal for these picture frames. Here is a simple design using bright, rainbow-colored yarn and just one style of stitch.

You will need

- Canvas • Tapestry yarn in rainbow colors
- Tapestry needle • Felt for backing • Sewing needle and thread • Thin cardboard

How to make a small frame

1 Cut a piece of canvas 5in (12.5cm) x 5in (12.5cm).

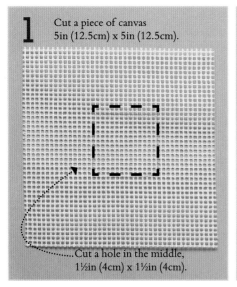

Cut a hole in the middle, 1½in (4cm) x 1½in (4cm).

2 Start stitching from the center. Change color for each row.

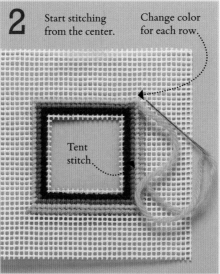

Tent stitch.

3 Cut the frame out of the canvas.

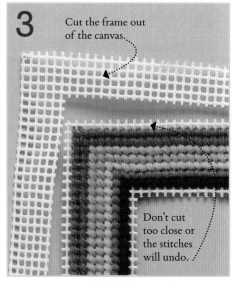

Don't cut too close or the stitches will undo.

4

Stitch over the rough edges.

5 Cut a piece of felt the same size as the frame.

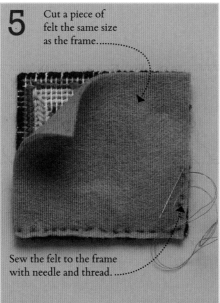

Sew the felt to the frame with needle and thread.

6

Cut the cardboard small enough to slide into the frame.

Glue your picture to the cardboard.

Hang 'em up

Hang your handiwork on the wall using these little tabs. Cut a piece of ribbon and sew in place on the felt layer of the frame.

Cut ribbon 1½in (4cm) long.

Use a sewing needle and thread to attach the tab to the felt.

Patchwork

To make patchwork, small, shaped pieces of fabric are sewn together in geometric patterns to create a large patterned cloth—a perfect way to use up scraps and recycle clothes.

Paper for patches

Each fabric patch will need to be attached to a paper shape. You can reuse old envelopes and magazines to make these. You will need a lot, since each patch has its own piece of paper, but they can be reused when the project is finished.

Isometric paper to create designs (see templates on page 62)

Patchwork fabric

Lightweight cotton is best for patchwork; don't use anything stretchy or too thick, since it will be difficult to make the patches even. Experiment with colors and patterns, too.

Tracing paper

Graph paper for patch designs

Sewing needle and pins

Sewing thread for basting fabric to paper patches and sewing patches together

Old envelopes are good for paper patches.

Cardboard for templates

Ruler for drawing and measuring templates

Templates

Cardboard from cereal boxes is ideal, but any cardboard that is easy to cut will do.

Pencil to draw around the shapes

How patchwork works

Every patch needs a piece of fabric and a paper shape. The paper is basted to the fabric, and then these patches are stitched together. The paper remains in the patch until you have finished. Templates made of cardboard are used to get the right size for the fabric and paper.

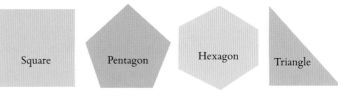

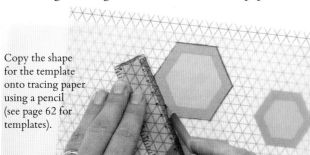

Square   Pentagon   Hexagon   Triangle

Patchwork pieces are based on these shapes.

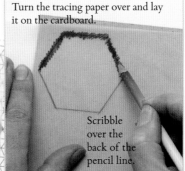

Turn the tracing paper over and lay it on the cardboard.

Scribble over the back of the pencil line.

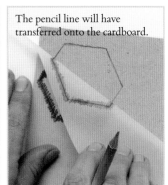

The pencil line will have transferred onto the cardboard.

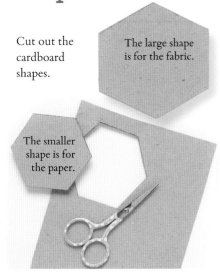

Copy the shape for the template onto tracing paper using a pencil (see page 62 for templates).

Templates

Cut out the cardboard shapes.

The large shape is for the fabric.

The smaller shape is for the paper.

Preparing the paper shapes

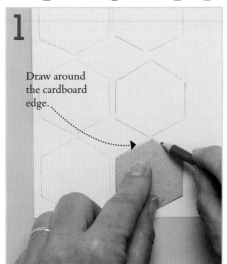

1

Draw around the cardboard edge.

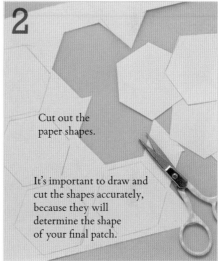

2

Cut out the paper shapes.

It's important to draw and cut the shapes accurately, because they will determine the shape of your final patch.

Preparing the fabric

Select some fabrics that work well together.

Use the large template for the fabric.

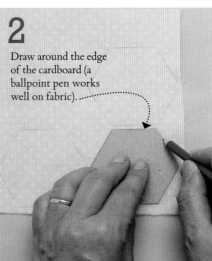

2

Draw around the edge of the cardboard (a ballpoint pen works well on fabric).

3

Cut out the fabric shapes.

Preparing the patches

1 Fold the fabric over the paper. ……

Carefully pin the paper in the center of the fabric.

REVERSE SIDE OF FABRIC

Hold the fabric in place as you stitch.

2 Use basting stitch to attach the fabric. ……

Stitch over the corner to hold it in place.

3 To finish, continue stitching to just past the knot.

Remove the pins.

A completed seven-patch block

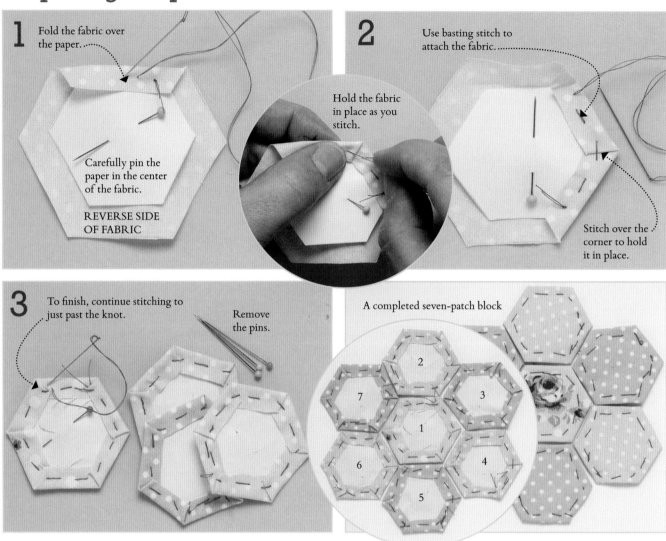

Sewing patches together

1 Place the patches together with their fronts facing each other.

Use tiny stitches to whipstitch the edges. ……

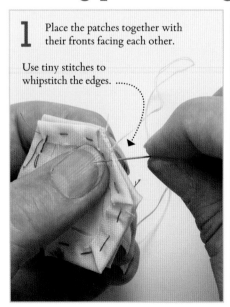

2 At the end of the patch, stitch back over your last few stitches to secure.

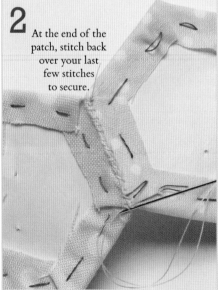

3 Continue stitching the rest of the patches together.

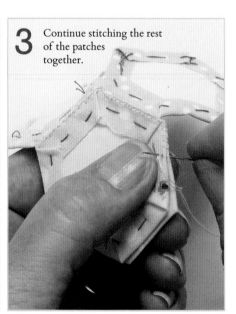

Removing the paper patch

When all the patches are sewn together, press them flat with an iron.

Cut the basting thread and pull it out.

Carefully remove the paper templates.

Pressing the patch

Once the paper has been removed, the patches will be flimsy and the folded seams will tend to unfold. To keep them in shape, press with a hot iron.

! BE CAREFUL—IRONS ARE HOT!

ASK AN ADULT FOR HELP.

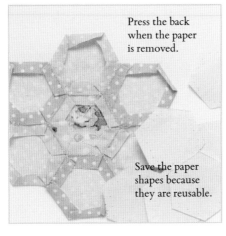

Press the back when the paper is removed.

Save the paper shapes because they are reusable.

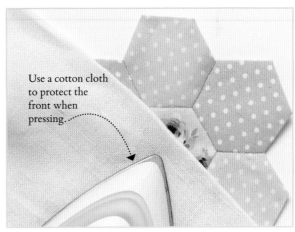

Use a cotton cloth to protect the front when pressing.

Patchwork pattern blocks

Triangles can be used to make up blocks of larger triangles or squares.

Blocks When patches are sewn together like this, they are known as blocks. These blocks can help when making large pieces. Placing the blocks in different ways creates all kinds of new designs.

Six-sided shapes, sewn together, make a seven-patch block.

Squares can be joined to make a nine-patch block.

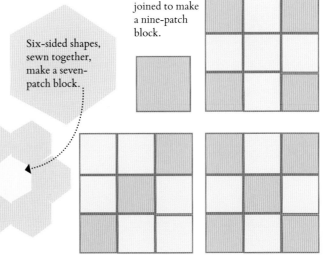

Squares and triangles

Lots of patterns can be made by placing blocks of triangles in different ways. Choose fabrics with very different, contrasting colors and patterns for more dramatic effects.

You will need

- 4 different fabric designs • Paper templates (see page 62) • Sewing thread and needle

Make a block

Make four triangular patches by using the template on page 62. You can use the graph paper.

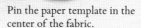

Pin the paper template in the center of the fabric.

Fold the fabric over the paper and sew in place.

Stitch the triangles together.

Make four triangles the same size.

Fold down all the pointed ends and pin them along the folded edge. Neatly sew all around the edge.

Make three more blocks in the same way.

Sew the four blocks together on the reverse side using small stitches.

Remove the paper and use an iron to press the reverse side flat.

Join blocks together

Turn each block around so the triangles match up differently.

Patchy cushions

Shaped like a honeycomb, these six-sided patches are sewn together to make a seven-patch block. Here, two blocks have been stitched together and stuffed to make cushions.

Make 2 x seven-patch blocks

To make the blocks, follow the steps on pages 24–27.

This design uses a different fabric for each patch.

To help flatten the fabric, iron the blocks before removing the paper.

How to make a pincushion

1 Remove the template paper.

Iron the fabric edges flat again at this stage.

2 Place the blocks with the wrong sides facing each other.

Whipstitch the edges together.

Leave an opening for the filling.

3

Fill the cushion, working the stuffing into the corners.

Neatly sew up the opening.

Little and Large

It's so simple; the size of the patch will make a smaller or larger cushion. Go to page 62 and try out some different-sized templates.

Match the patch

The seven-patch blocks can be sewn together to become a larger piece of fabric, such as a quilt for your bed.

Appliqué

What is appliqué? Well, it's pictures and patterns made by sewing small fabric shapes to a piece of material. Motifs can be used like patches to dress up clothing. Sewing stitches can be invisible, but embroidery stitches are a perfect way to add decoration.

Tracing paper

Transfer paper

Tracing paper

Use this for copying an image and transferring the outline as a pattern for your piece of fabric.

Transfer paper

Used in dressmaking and craft projects, this paper has a glued backing that, when heated, can be used to attach motifs to the fabric items.

Fabrics

Lightweight cotton fabric is best for appliqué. In addition to coming in an array of colors and patterns, it is easy to cut and shape. The cut edges will fray, but stitching the edges and using adhesive transfer paper will help. Avoid stretchy fabric, since this can distort the motif shapes.

Buttons for decoration

Needles and pins

Embroidery thread

Sewing thread

Scissors for cutting out shapes

Pencil for tracing motifs

Felt fabric

Felt will not fray like other fabrics because of the way it is made. This makes it ideal for appliqué, since even the smallest motifs will keep their shape.

Transferring designs using transfer paper

What is transfer paper?

Transfer paper is a handy way to attach motifs to the fabric items you want to decorate. It's like tracing paper with glue on one side. It works in two steps: first, you stick the paper shape to your motif fabric; next, you iron the motif to the fabric you are decorating. Follow the manufacturer's instructions.

1

Place the transfer paper over the image you have chosen and trace over the outline with a pencil.

Cut the pieces of transfer paper so they are slightly bigger than the image.

2

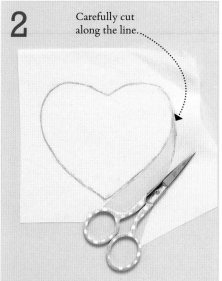

Carefully cut along the line.

3

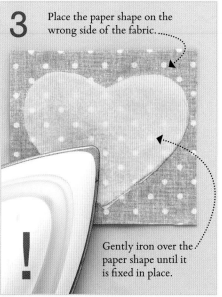

Place the paper shape on the wrong side of the fabric.

Gently iron over the paper shape until it is fixed in place.

!

4

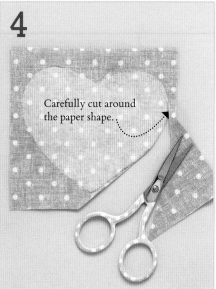

Carefully cut around the paper shape.

5

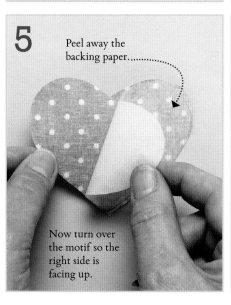

Peel away the backing paper.

Now turn over the motif so the right side is facing up.

6

Carefully position the motif where you want it to go.

Gently iron all over the motif until it is stuck down.

!

Using an iron

CAREFUL— IRONS ARE HOT!

ASK AN ADULT FOR HELP.

• The iron will need to be hot to make the transfer paper work effectively.

• PLEASE NOTE: Some fabrics will melt if you iron them. Place a piece of cotton cloth over the fabric motif before ironing to keep this from happening.

Paper patterns

Fabric motifs can be attached by simply pinning them directly to the base fabric. Trace over the image and cut out the shape, then, using the tracing-paper shape, cut out the fabric motif.

Tracing paper template

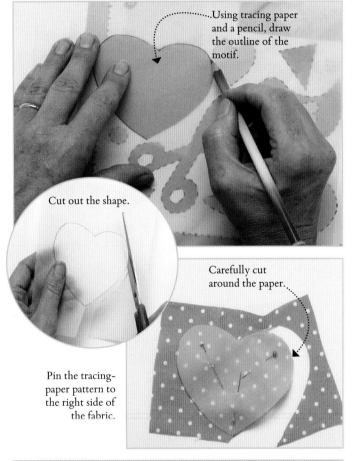

Using tracing paper and a pencil, draw the outline of the motif.

Cut out the shape.

Carefully cut around the paper.

Pin the tracing-paper pattern to the right side of the fabric.

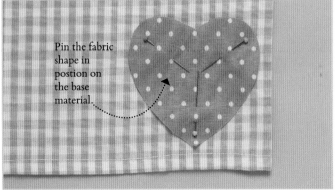

Pin the fabric shape in postion on the base material.

Decorative stitching

Stitches used for attaching the motifs can be tiny and invisible, using sewing thread, or they can be made to be part of the design. Try out the stitches from the Embroidery pages of the book (pages 6–15). Here are three decorative ways of making stitches part of the design using embroidery thread.

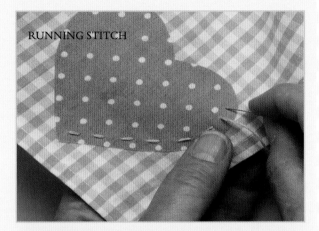

RUNNING STITCH

STRAIGHT STITCH

BLANKET STITCH

This stitch is useful if the edges of fabric are fraying.

Ready-made motifs

Look for fabric with big, bold designs because these make perfect motifs.

DIY shapes

Design your own motifs. If you can't find a design you like or you have a picture in mind, draw the design on paper and use this as your pattern. Cut out the shapes and pin them to the fabric, then cut out to make the fabric shapes.

Handy tip

If you don't have any adhesive transfer paper, simply cut out the shapes, pin them to the backing material, and sew them in place.

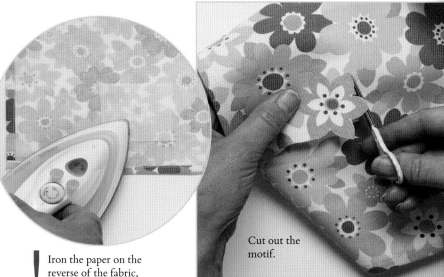

! Iron the paper on the reverse of the fabric, ■ over the motif.

Cut out the motif.

! Iron the motif in position.

Cupcake bag

Create a delicious cupcake bag using felt and buttons. First, draw your design on paper, then cut it out to use as the pattern. Felt is great because it doesn't fray at the edges.

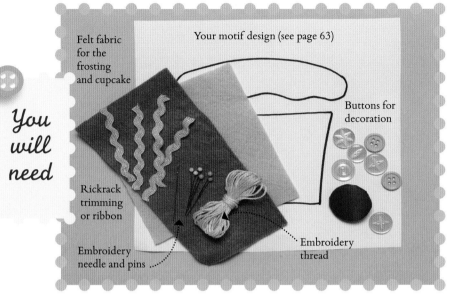

You will need

Felt fabric for the frosting and cupcake

Your motif design (see page 63)

Buttons for decoration

Rickrack trimming or ribbon

Embroidery needle and pins

Embroidery thread

Bag size

Cut out a piece of fabric 8in (20cm) x 16in (42cm). Position the motif in the top half of the fabric, as shown below. Remember to allow space for the seams and for turning the fabric at the top of the bag.

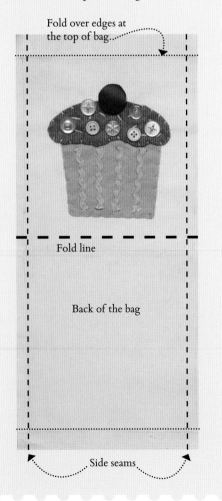

Fold over edges at the top of bag

Fold line

Back of the bag

Side seams

How to make the motif

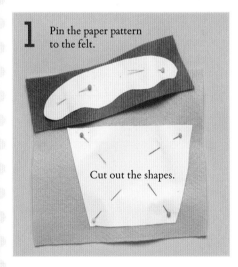

1 Pin the paper pattern to the felt.

Cut out the shapes.

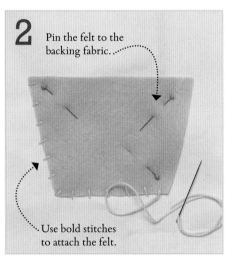

2 Pin the felt to the backing fabric.

Use bold stitches to attach the felt.

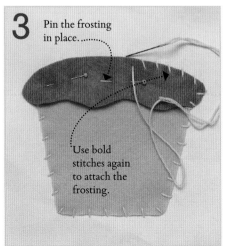

3 Pin the frosting in place.

Use bold stitches again to attach the frosting.

4 Start to decorate the cupcake with stitches for sprinkles.

Stitch the trimming or ribbon to the cupcake with running stitch.

Ready-made

If you already have a bag, you can decorate that instead. Just follow the motif step-by-steps in the same way.

Use ribbon or trimming to create the sides of a cupcake liner.

Collect buttons to decorate your work.

Make a bag

Fold the fabric in half, right sides facing. Fold the tops of the bag over and stitch in place on either side. Sew together the sides using backstitch. Finally, pin the handles on and sew them in position.

Fold over the fabric at the top and sew up the sides.

Pin the handles to the bag and sew them in place.

Birds, bunting, and buttons

Make beautiful crafty boxes.
By using even the smallest scraps of fabric, appliqué is a perfect way to create patches to decorate boxes and bags. These sewing-theme motifs are a lovely finish to your craft kit.

Trace the shapes from this page onto the transfer paper.

You will need

- Adhesive transfer paper
- Pencil • Iron • Backing fabric • Scraps of fabric for shapes • Rickrack trimming
- Sewing thread and needle

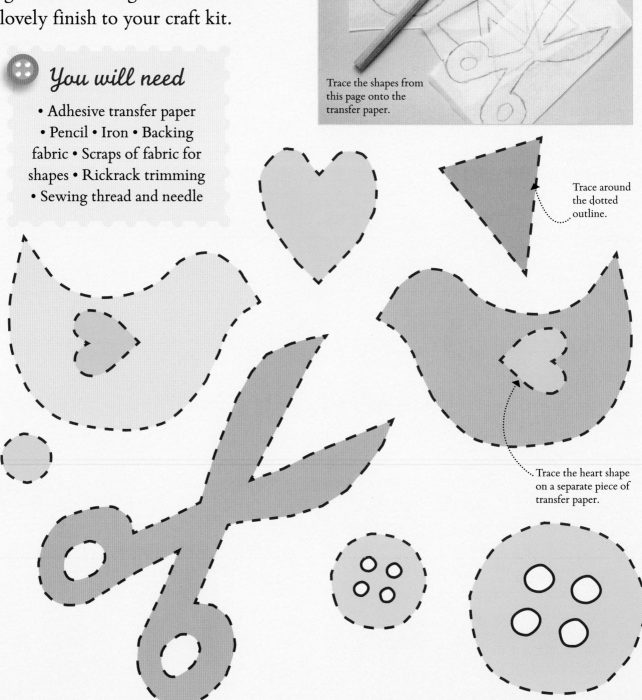

Trace around the dotted outline.

Trace the heart shape on a separate piece of transfer paper.

Position the shapes

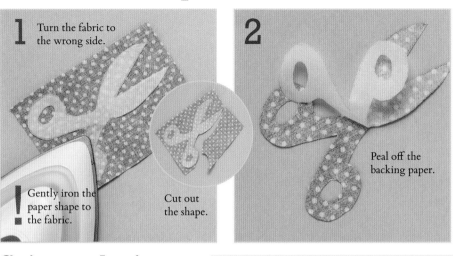

1 Turn the fabric to the wrong side.

! Gently iron the paper shape to the fabric.

Cut out the shape.

2 Peal off the backing paper.

3 Place the shape right side up on the fabric.

! Gently iron the shape onto the fabric.

Scissor design

Collect up all the pieces to decorate the fabric patch. The rickrack border and very small scraps of fabric do not need the adhesive backing.

Sew the shape to the fabric patch with running stitch.

The stitches are for decoration, so keep them neat and even.

Rickrack border

Small shapes and buttons can be sewn directly onto the patch.

Position the rickrack border with pins, then sew in place.

Match the ends of the rickrack to look neat.

Carefully snip holes for the fabric buttons.

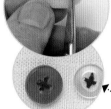

Sew on the buttons with different-colored thread.

Birds and bunting

Cut out a piece of fabric for the patch.

Cut out the fabric shapes.

Prepare the shapes to be ironed on (as above).

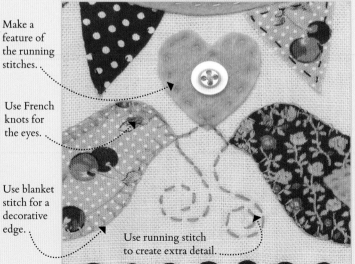

Make a feature of the running stitches.

Use French knots for the eyes.

Use blanket stitch for a decorative edge.

Use running stitch to create extra detail.

Pincushion

This big button motif makes a pretty pincushion or button-box lid.

Big button design

Cut out the fabric for the patch.

Iron on the motif and sew in place.

Use bold stitches.

Finish it with a rickrack border.

Craft in a bag,

Here, a patch has been sewn to a small tote bag— a handy place to keep your craft materials.

More ideas
The finished patches can be applied to all kinds of surfaces. Either stitch them to fabric, like this bag, or glue them onto a box lid.

Knitting

Two needles and a ball of yarn are all you need to start knitting. Work the stitches from one needle to the other and see the fabric grow.

KNITTING RULES
There are no set rules about how to use the yarn and needle—knitters all around the world use them in very different ways. The following pages show two methods, one of which is often preferred by left-handers.

Knitting needles

Knitting needles are available in many different sizes, from very narrow ones for fine work to very thick ones that produce a chunky knit. The projects that follow use a medium-sized needle.

Tapestry needle for sewing up projects

Knitting spool

Also known as French knitting and i-Cord knitting, this gadget knits yarn into long braids that can be used with all kinds of projects.

The pin is used to work the yarn over the top of hooks on the spool.

US 6 (4mm) knitting needles

Stitch types

There are two stitch types used in the projects that follow, knit stitch and purl stitch. Knitting patterns shorten the names as shown below:

k = knit
p = purl
st = stitch

Braids made with the knitting spool

Double-knit (DK) yarn

Yarns

The many different types of yarn are described by their "weight." The yarn used for the projects that follow is a double-knit, or DK, weight and made of either wool or acrylic. Other yarns are known as 4-ply and chunky. Each yarn will produce a different feel to the fabric.

How to get started

Knitting is produced with two needles, one held in each hand. To begin, you need to make stitches—this is called casting on. You will need to cast on the number of stitches required in the pattern. The stitches that are being worked will be on the left-hand needle and the ones you have made will go on the right.

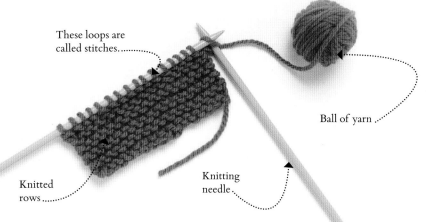

These loops are called stitches...........

Ball of yarn ....

Knitted rows ....

Knitting needle ....

Slipknot   The first stitch on the needle is knotted so the yarn stays on.

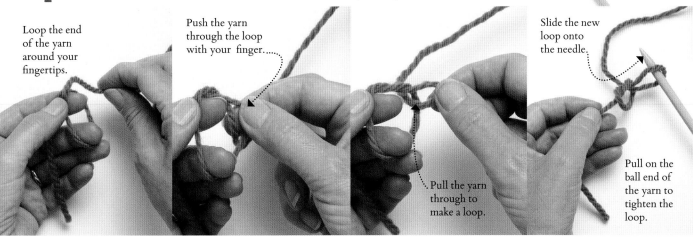

Loop the end of the yarn around your fingertips.

Push the yarn through the loop with your finger....

Pull the yarn through to make a loop.

Slide the new loop onto the needle.

Pull on the ball end of the yarn to tighten the loop.

Casting on   There are many ways to cast on. This method uses your thumb.

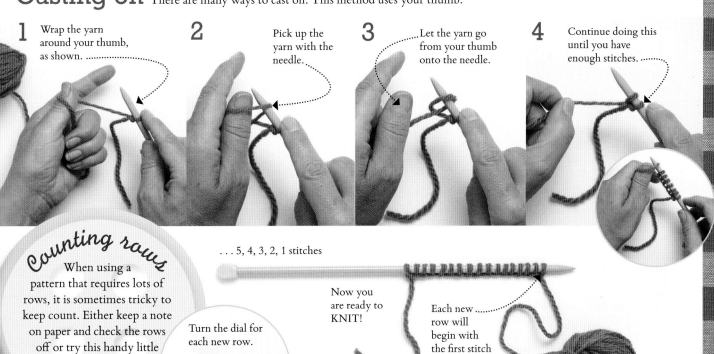

1 Wrap the yarn around your thumb, as shown. ....

2 Pick up the yarn with the needle. ....

3 Let the yarn go from your thumb onto the needle. ....

4 Continue doing this until you have enough stitches. ....

Counting rows
When using a pattern that requires lots of rows, it is sometimes tricky to keep count. Either keep a note on paper and check the rows off or try this handy little gadget that fits on the end of your needle.

Turn the dial for each new row.

. . . 5, 4, 3, 2, 1 stitches

Now you are ready to KNIT!

Each new ....
row will begin with the first stitch on the right.

Knit stitch

Also called plain stitch, this stitch is thought to be the easiest to make and is certainly a useful basic stitch for simple projects.

For knit stitch, the right-hand needle goes to the back of the stitch.

The yarn also goes at the back.

Method 1 (This is the English method.)

1 Hold the knitting with your hands in this position.

Take the yarn around the back.

Place the needle in the back of the stitch.

2 Wrap the yarn under and around the needle from right to left.

Method 2 (This is the Continental method; it is often helpful for left-handers.)

1 Place the yarn between the fingers of your left hand.

2 Use your middle finger to move the yarn.

Take the yarn around the front of the needle.

Your index finger and thumb are used to hold the knitting in place.

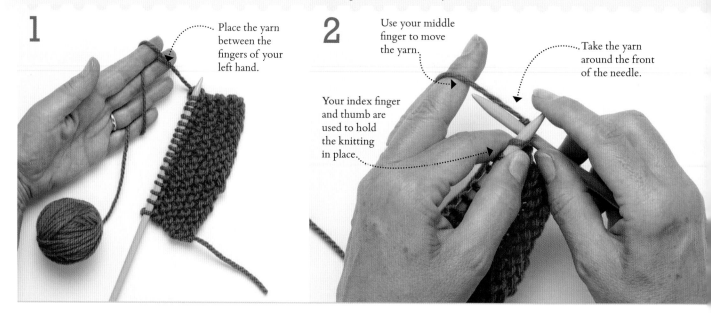

Garter Stitch

Garter stitch isn't an actual stitch, but the name of the pattern given to a piece of knitting where every row is knitted in knit stitch. It has ridges on both sides.

Garter stitch is also made if you knit every row in purl stitch.

3 Pull on the yarn and move the needle from the back to the front.

4 The right needle is now on top of the left one and has taken the stitch with it.

5 Slide the top needle to the right. The stitch will now be transferred onto the right needle, completing the stitch.

Begin the next stitch as in step 1.

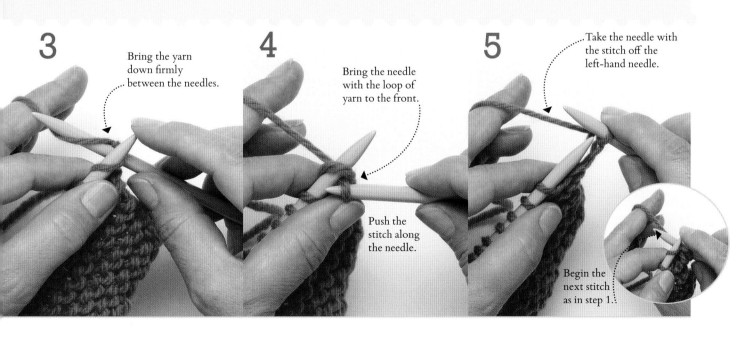

3 Bring the yarn down firmly between the needles.

4 Bring the needle with the loop of yarn to the front.

Push the stitch along the needle.

5 Take the needle with the stitch off the left-hand needle.

Begin the next stitch as in step 1.

Making shapes

You can shape the knitting by adding (increasing) or taking away (decreasing) stitches. There are many different ways to do this, but here are two simple methods that you can use for the projects in this book.

INCREASE SHAPE

...An extra stitch has been made at the beginning and the end of each row.

Two stitches have been knitted together at the beginning and end of each row...

DECREASE SHAPE

Make a stitch—increasing

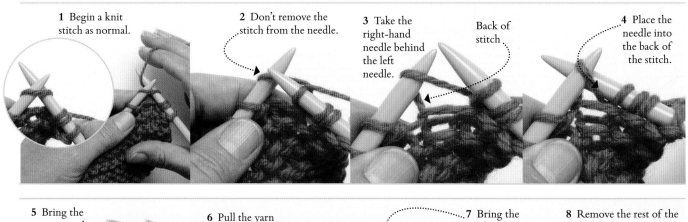

1 Begin a knit stitch as normal.

2 Don't remove the stitch from the needle.

3 Take the right-hand needle behind the left needle.

Back of stitch

4 Place the needle into the back of the stitch.

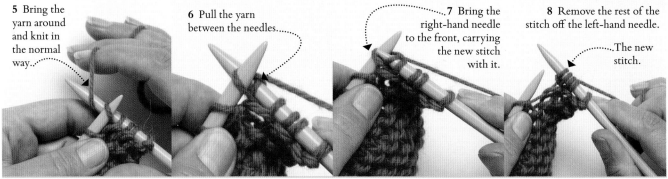

5 Bring the yarn around and knit in the normal way.

6 Pull the yarn between the needles.

7 Bring the right-hand needle to the front, carrying the new stitch with it.

8 Remove the rest of the stitch off the left-hand needle.

...The new stitch.

Knit two together—decreasing

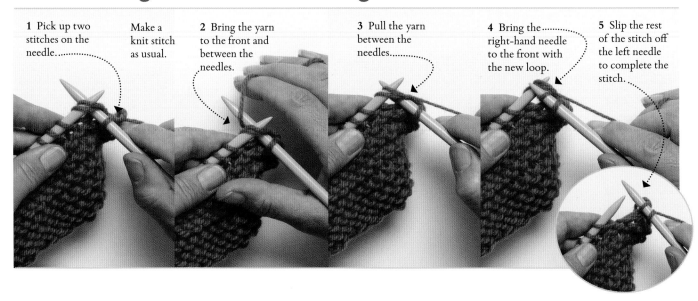

1 Pick up two stitches on the needle.

Make a knit stitch as usual.

2 Bring the yarn to the front and between the needles.

3 Pull the yarn between the needles.

4 Bring the right-hand needle to the front with the new loop.

5 Slip the rest of the stitch off the left needle to complete the stitch.

Join new yarn

1 Tie the new yarn to the old yarn with a loose knot.

2 Slide the knot up the yarn to the needle.

3 Continue knitting as usual.

Knit in new color

Here, the knitting is shown on the reverse side. Join the new yarn as shown (left). To neaten the loose ends of both colors, gather them up with the working yarn as you knit.

Casting off

1 Begin the row by knitting two stitches.

2 Pick up the first stitch with the left needle.

3 Carry this first stitch over the second stitch and over the end of the needle.

4 Repeat steps 1–3...

5 ... until one stitch remains. Open up the loop.

6 Cut the yarn and place the end in the loop...

7 Pull the yarn to close the loop.

Neaten ends

(Sewing in ends when adding new yarn or tidying the loose ends of finished pieces).

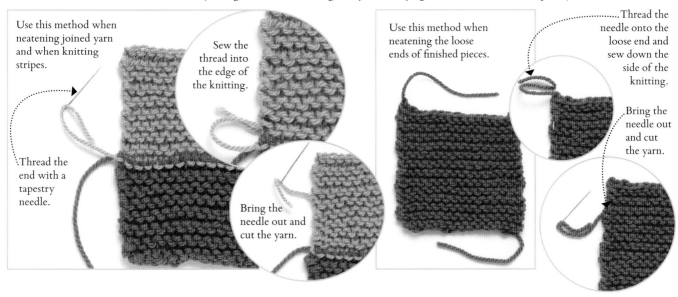

Use this method when neatening joined yarn and when knitting stripes.

Thread the end with a tapestry needle.

Sew the thread into the edge of the knitting.

Bring the needle out and cut the yarn.

Use this method when neatening the loose ends of finished pieces.

Thread the needle onto the loose end and sew down the side of the knitting.

Bring the needle out and cut the yarn.

Just knit it!

Master knit stitch and you can make plenty of things just by using one stitch. Here's a chance for you to practice your skills.

You will need

- US 6 (4mm) knitting needles
- Double knit yarn

HAT
2 x 1¾ oz (50 gram) balls

SCARF
2 x 1¾ oz (50 gram) balls

BAG
1 x 1¾ oz (50 gram) ball

STRAP
1 x 1¾ oz (50 gram) ball

RIBBON
1 x 1¾ oz (50 gram) ball

Hat
Cast on 50 stitches. Row 1 knit stitch. Continue using knit stitch until the piece measures 16in (40cm). Cast off.

Scarf
Cast on 24 stitches. Row 1 knit stitch. Continue using knit stitch until the piece measures 36in (90cm). Cast off.

Bag
Cast on 14 stitches. Row 1 knit stitch. Continue using knit stitch until the piece measures 10in (24cm). Cast off.

Bag strap
Cast on 3 stitches. Row 1 knit stitch. Continue using knit stitch until the piece measures 30in (76cm). Cast off.

Ribbon
Cast on 6 stitches. Row 1 knit stitch. Continue using knit stitch until the piece measures 16in (40cm). Cast off.

HAT

RIBBON

SCARF

BAG STRAP

BAG

How to make hats, scarves, bags, and bows

Start by sewing the loose ends into the pieces of knitting (see page 47). Use a tapestry needle and the yarn that you used to make the item to sew the pieces together. When you have finished, decorate the pieces with buttons.

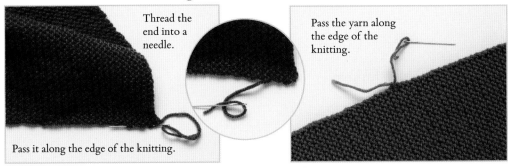

Thread the end into a needle.

Pass the yarn along the edge of the knitting.

Pass it along the edge of the knitting.

Make a hat

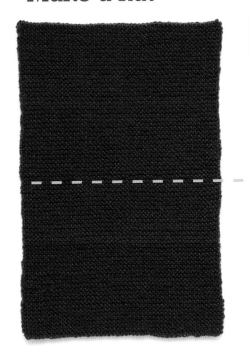

Fold the knitting in half.

Place the edges together.

Pin in place and begin to sew.

Turn the hat inside out and fold up the edge to make the hat smaller.

Make a bag

Fold the knitting in half.

Pin the sides together.

Stitch together using backstitch.

Attach the strap to the edge of the bag.

Making tassels

Sew in the loose ends where the yarn is joined.

The thickness of the tassel can vary, depending on how many loops of yarn you make. Cut a piece of cardboard twice the length you'd like your tassels to be. You will need a crochet hook to fix them into place.

Tie the yarn to the cardboard and wind it around 8 times.

Cut the yarn at the top and bottom.

Fold two strands in half.

1 Push a large crochet hook through the edge of the knitting.

Hook up the two folded strands of yarn.

2 Carefully take the hook back through the knitting, pulling the yarn with it.

3 Remove the hook.

4 Place the yarn ends through the loop to create a loose knot.

5 Space the tassels evenly across the end of the scarf.

Cut the tassels to the same length once they are all in place.

Make a bow

You can also simply tie your ribbon into a bow.

Fold one end over across the middle.

Fold the other end over across the first.

Sew in place with a couple of stitches.

Purl stitch

It's all up front with purl stitch. The yarn is worked from the front and the needle goes in the front of the stitch.

For purl stitch, the needle goes in the front of the stitch.

The yarn also goes at the front, too.

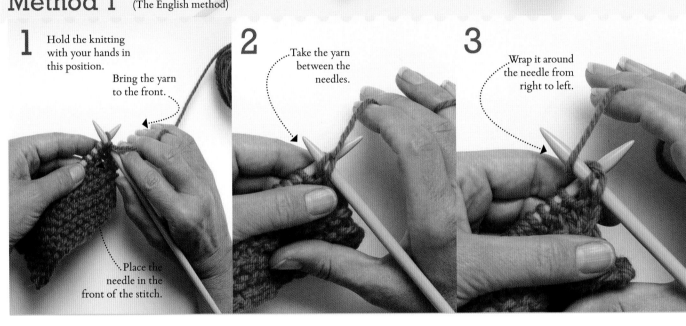

Method 1 (The English method)

1 Hold the knitting with your hands in this position.

Bring the yarn to the front.

Place the needle in the front of the stitch.

2 Take the yarn between the needles.

3 Wrap it around the needle from right to left.

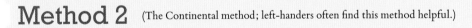

Method 2 (The Continental method; left-handers often find this method helpful.)

1 Place the right-hand needle in the front of the stitch.

Wind the yarn around your fingers.

2 Bring the yarn around the front of the needle.

3 Pull the yarn down with your index finger.

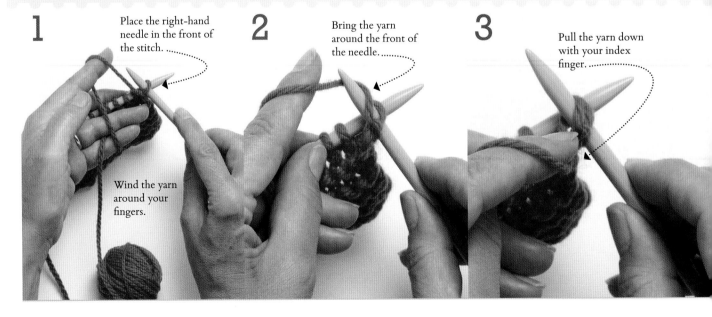

Purl stitch + Knit stitch = Stockinette stitch

STOCKINETTE STITCH isn't an actual stitch at all. Instead, it is made by working a knit row, then a purl row, a knit row, then a purl row, and so on. The result is a smooth front to the knitting and a ridged back.

FRONT
The knit-stitch side

BACK
The purl-stitch side

4 Pull on the yarn and move the needle from front to back ...

5 ... taking the stitch with it.

6 Take the rest of the yarn off the needle to complete the stitch.

Begin the next stitch as in Step 1.

4 Bring the right-hand needle from front to back, taking the yarn with it.

5 Pull the rest of the stitch off the needle.

6 Now you are ready to begin the next stitch, starting at Step 1 again.

Knitted roses

Make a bunch of colorful, woolly roses. These simple knitted shapes are twisted and curled to form a rose flower. It only takes a small amount of yarn to make one, so it's a neat way to use up any scraps.

You will need

- US 6 (4mm) knitting needles
- 15ft (5m) yarn • Felt
- Tapestry needle
- Sewing needle and thread

Rose pattern

Cast on 32 stitches
Row 1: knit st
Row 2: purl st
Row 3: knit st
Row 4: purl st
Decrease
Row 5: knit two together to end of row =16 st
Row 6: knit two together to end of row = 8 st
Row 7: knit two together to end of row = 4 st
Row 8: knit two together = 2 st
Cast off

How to make a rose

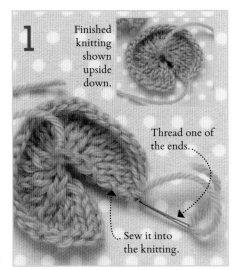

1 Finished knitting shown upside down.
Thread one of the ends...
...Sew it into the knitting.

2 Thread the yarn end from the center.

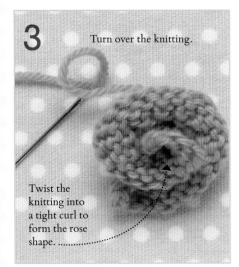

3 Turn over the knitting.
Twist the knitting into a tight curl to form the rose shape. ...

4 Sew the outer side of the curl to the back of the rose to hold it in position.

5 Cut out some felt leaves.
Sew the leaf to the back of the rose.
Whipstitch the edge of the felt with small neat stitches. ....

Rosy brooch

Your rose makes a pretty brooch. Sew a safety pin to the felt leaves, or sew the roses directly onto your bags, either on their own or in bunches of three.

Crochet

It's all about pulling loops
through loops to create a piece of fabric, working with only one stitch at a time—now all you need is a hook and some yarn.

US 7 (4.5mm) crochet hook

US L-11 (8mm) crochet hook

Crochet hooks

Hooks are available in many different size—the larger the hook, the larger the stitch. The projects that follow are made using a medium-sized US 7 (4.5mm) hook. If you use a metal hook, the yarn will move more freely, compared to a plastic one.

Yarn

The projects in this book are made with cotton yarn in a double-knit (DK) weight.

Cotton yarn is not fluffy like some wool yarns. This makes it perfect when learning how to crochet, because it's easy to see the stitches.

Stitch types

The Bag of stripes project in this book features just two basic crochet stitches: chain stitch and single crochet. These stitch names may sometimes appear shortened in crochet patterns that you find elsewhere.

ch = chain stitch
sc = single crochet (UK = double crochet)

How to get started

Working loop

Crochet hook

Stitches

Rows

Unlike knitting, which uses two needles and where the working stitches are all on the needles, crochet is worked with a hook, and only one stitch is made at a time.

This has been worked in single crochet.

HOW TO HOLD the work

Wrap the yarn around your left hand, as shown here.

Hold the hook in your right hand.

Slipknot

The first stitch on the hook is knotted so the yarn stays on.

1 Make a loop with the end of the yarn around your fingertips.

2 Push the yarn through the loop with your index finger.

3 Pull the yarn through.

4 Transfer the loop onto the hook and pull gently on the yarn.

Foundation chain

The number of stitches on the chain will determine the width of the crochet fabric.

1 Hold the slipknot firmly between finger and thumb.

2 Push the hook under the yarn and catch it with the hook.

3 Pull the hook back through the stitch.

4 The stitch is complete.

NOW REPEAT STEPS 1–4 to continue the chain.

Make as many chain stitches as the pattern requires.

This foundation chain has 10 stitches—count the "V" shapes.

1 2 3 4 5 6 7 8 9 10

The back of the stitches will look very knobbly.

Single crochet

How to start Once you have made the foundation chain, you are ready to start crocheting. With any type of stitch you use, you will need to make chain stitches at the beginning of each row, so that your work is brought up to the right height.

First row in single crochet

Single crochet This basic stitch is useful for all kinds of projects. It produces a close, firm fabric.

Chain stitch At the beginning of the second row, make one chain stitch. This means when you begin to work across the row you will begin at the right height.

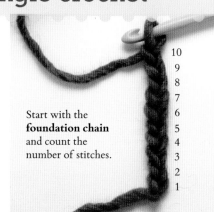

Start with the **foundation chain** and count the number of stitches.

2 YARN-OVER

Push the hook underneath and around the yarn.

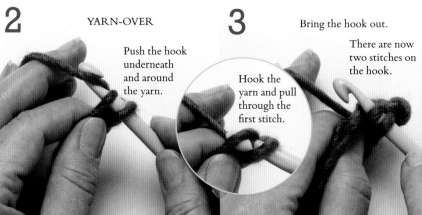

3

Bring the hook out.

There are now two stitches on the hook.

Hook the yarn and pull through the first stitch.

4

Push the hook underneath and around the yarn.

YARN-OVER

Hook the yarn and pull through both stitches.

Second row in single crochet

(Use this method for all the single crochet rows from now onward.)

1

Begin the row with a **chain stitch** so there are 11 stitches.

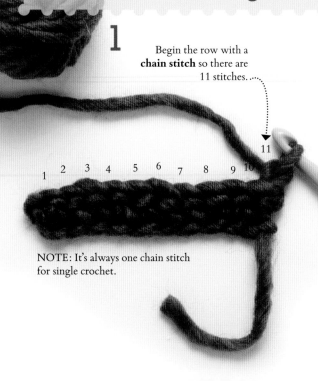

NOTE: It's always one chain stitch for single crochet.

2 YARN-OVER

Push the hook under the "V" of the second stitch (10th stitch).

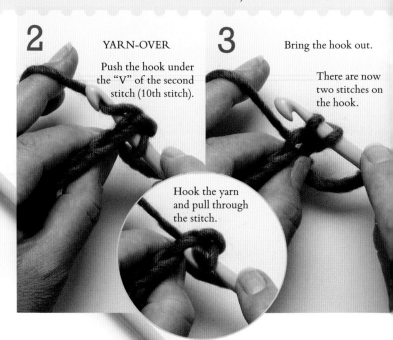

Hook the yarn and pull through the stitch.

3

Bring the hook out.

There are now two stitches on the hook.

1

At the beginning of Row 1 make a **chain stitch.**

1 2 3 4 5 6 7 8 9 10 11

There are now 11 stitches;
count the "V"s.

10

5 6 7 8 9

Push the hook into
the center of the
10th stitch (the
second from
the hook).

5

Now, one stitch is
left on the hook.

The **single
crochet** stitch
is complete.

REPEAT
STEPS 1–5
to the end
of the row.

10 9 8 7 6 5 4 3 2 1

The first row is
complete—with
10 stitches.

Turn the work to get ready
for the next row.

4 YARN-OVER

5

The stitch
is complete.
There is
now only
one stitch
left on the
hook.

Hook the
yarn and pull
through both
stitches.

Continue single crochet
stitches to the end of
the row.

10 9 8 7 6 5 4 3 2 1

The row is now complete. Turn
the work over and begin the next
row and REPEAT STEPS 1–5.

Bags of stripes

Changing colors is a fun way to liven up a simple strip of single crochet. A length of crochet is useful for lots of projects; here it's a handy bag.

You will need

- Cotton yarn in various colors
- US 7 (4.5mm) crochet hook
- Tapestry needle • Button

How to change colors

Crochet to the end of the row. Turn the work as usual, then cut off the old yarn, leaving a tail about 4in (10cm) long. Loop the new color over the hook, leaving a tail about 4in (10cm) long and pull it through the loop on the hook to make a stitch. Tug on the ends to pull the yarn tight. Continue working in new colors. Start the first stitch as chain stitch.

Neaten the loose ends by sewing them along the edge of the work.

Thread the ends onto the tapestry needle.

BAG PATTERN

Foundation chain: 16 stitches.
Row 1: Make 1 chain stitch, work 16 stitches in single crochet.
Continue working rows in single crochet, changing colors to create stripes.
In this design, the stripes are 3 to 4 rows deep, but the number of stripes is up to you. This length of crochet measures 12in (30cm).

Fold the work over, leaving room at the top for the flap.

Stitch the two edges together using whipstitch.

Sew up both sides; turn the work inside out.

Cut a piece of yarn 4in (10cm).

MAKE A BUTTON LOOP
Push the hook through the crochet, loop the yarn over the hook, and pull the hook back through the crochet. Finish the loop and sew on the button.

Place the ends through the loop and tie a knot to create a loop for the button.

Balls of yarn
Here is a collection of cotton yarn, double knit (DK) weight. To make the striped bag, use up leftover lengths.

Templates

1 Place tracing paper over the shape and use a pencil to copy it.

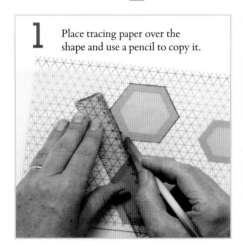

2 Turn the tracing paper over.

Scribble over the pencil line.

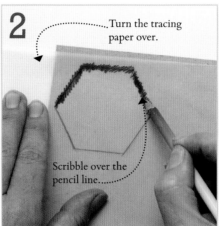

3 The pencil line tranfers to the cardboard.

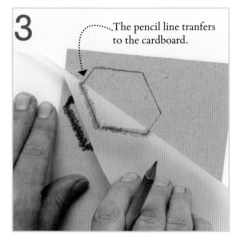

Transferring designs

Follow steps 1–3 to transfer the patchwork designs onto paper or cardboard.

THE CUPCAKE MOTIFS Because these designs aren't symmetrical, trace the shape on both sides at Step 1. This way, when the paper is turned over, the design will be the right way around.

Large cushion
Six-sided cushion, pages 30–31

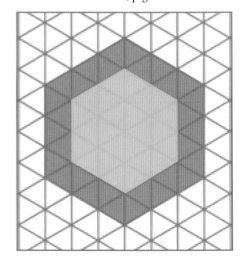

Small pincushion
Six-sided cushion, pages 30–31

Triangle patchwork
Squares and triangles, pages 28–29

Cupcake

Cupcake motif, pages 36–37

Index

Acknowledgments

Dorling Kindersley would like to thank:
Gemma Fletcher and Rosie Levine for design assistance;
David Fentiman for editorial assistance; Penny Arlon for
proofreading; Ray Williams for production help.

All images © Dorling Kindersley
For further information see: www.dkimages.com